Introducing Jewelry Making

Introducing Jewelry Making
John Crawford

B. T. Batsford Limited, London
Watson-Guptill Publications, New York

© John Crawford 1969
First published 1969
Reprinted 1972
Reprinted 1974

ISBN 0 7134 2405 2

Library of Congress Catalog Card Number 69-10796
Printed and bound in Great Britain by
William Clowes & Sons, Limited
London, Beccles and Colchester
for the publishers
B. T. Batsford Limited, 4 Fitzhardinge Street, London, W.1 and
Watson-Guptill Publications,
One Astor Plaza, New York, NY 10036

Contents

Acknowledgment

I wish to express my thanks to the many people who have given help in the production of this book.

I am indebted to Dr D. M. McIntosh, CBE, MA, BSc, MEd, PhD, LLD, FRSE, FEIS, Principal of Moray House College of Education, Edinburgh, for permission to use the photographs of work by College students.

I am extremely grateful to my colleague Raymond Townsend whose photographs are used throughout the book.

My thanks also to the National Museum of Antiquities of Scotland for permission to reproduce the illustrations 1, 2, 3, 46, 86, and to the Royal Scottish Museum for permission to use figures 14, 15, 16, 17, 32, 108, 115, and 118.

Edinburgh 1968   J.C.

Introduction

This book does not pretend to be a handbook on the making of jewelry but is an attempt to introduce the craft as an adjunct to other art and craft activities and to give a basis on which to start such activities in schools and colleges or indeed by interested individuals.

Art and craft techniques increase and decrease in popularity through the ages as educational fashion swings towards some chosen activity only to discard it in favour of some seemingly more relevant form after only a short time.

This is reasonable provided the teachers concerned are looking for a craft which will be of use to the student in giving him an opportunity to develop along genuine creative lines and not just make him learn a series of skills which will produce a particular object.

What is necessary then, is an activity that allows scope for the creation of individual art works by the student and at the same time teaches or gives opportunity for the development of such things as basic design and an appreciation of colour, surface texture, form and the linking of these things with the business of living.

It would appear then that, along with other crafts, jewelry satisfies all these criteria and has the added advantage that decoration of the body with small precious objects was and still is one of mans' basic primitive urges.

The acquisition and wearing of precious or decorative pieces of stone, bone, or metal for an amuletic function in protecting the wearer by means of charms or merely to denote rank and wealth is almost as old as the first signs of civilisation in primitive man.

That this urge exists today is beyond doubt and therefore it would seem only sensible to exploit it in children and students and further a genuine creative activity which involves so many aspects of art education.

The materials of jewelry making are and always have been extremely varied. It is this variety that gives scope to the imagination and indeed it may lead the student to the study of some other aspect of the chosen substance, which may be equally valuable to the educational process.

Traditionally, metals of various kinds, stones, wood, ivory, bone and vitreous enamels have been used in the creation of jewelry, and today, with the introduction of plastics, many other materials are being used.

With this vast area of study it is almost impossible to cover all aspects and therefore as the use of the word traditionally suggests, an historical basis has been taken for each of the sections covered in the following pages.

The metal used for almost all of the pieces illustrated is copper which still remains relatively inexpensive and all the other materials suggested can either be purchased very cheaply or found easily in their natural state.

Section 1

Materials

The greater part of the book deals with the making of simple metal jewelry and a reasonably soft metal is most suitable for this purpose. Copper and silver are two of the most malleable and ductile metals and of these copper is the least expensive and therefore the most suitable for use in schools and colleges as a beginners material.

Copper can be bought as both sheet and wire as well as in many other forms such as pipes and tubes of various dimensions and is easily available in most localities. Although cheap to buy, copper is extremely attractive in colour and can be finished in a number of ways to give a tremendous variety of texture.

Since 8000 B.C. copper has been used in its pure state and as an alloy with other metals. Early man found it both decorative, because of its rich red colour and functional since it is both malleable and durable. Copper jewelery, dating from many different periods, can be found in most museums.

History also provides us with many other materials which can be re-interpreted for use today and museum study is a first-class source of inspiration to the student. Primitive craftsmen with no knowledge of metal used a fantastic variety of materials such as seeds, bamboo, reeds and twigs as well as ivory from elephant and walrus and bones and teeth from other animals.

Shells, coloured stones, decorative pieces of wood and many other materials were sawn or drilled using extremely primitive tools.

Using today's equipment all these materials can be exploited and the search for others of use in the production of jewelry can be rewarding both in the training of the imagination and in the observation of both natural and man-made objects.

The illustrations of the bone beads and tusk pendants from Skara Brae give some idea of the type of jewelry produced by Neolithic man who had no metal tools to help him.

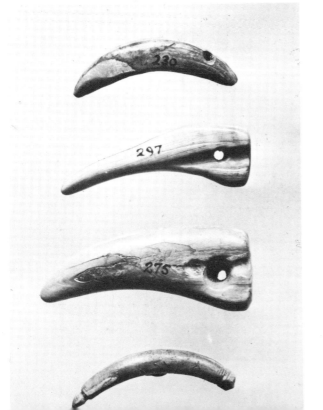

1 Necklace of bone beads and animal teeth found at Skara Brae, Orkney
2 Boars Tusks drilled for use as pendants. Skara Brae, Orkney

3 Bone marked and grooved ready for cutting to produce bone beads similar to those in the necklace in figure 1 Skara Brae, Orkney

The bone in figure 3 is marked out and partially cut ready to produce bone beads. This would have been done using only flint knives, which accounts for the whittled appearance of each cut. However the bones in figure 117 (section 6) have been cut with a hacksaw and each bead will require to be rubbed with sandpaper or against a lump of sandstone to give it the rounded appearance of the primitive examples.

Inexpensive materials do not necessitate the production of 'cheap' jewelry and in fact the very simplification of the work, due to lack of tools and equipment and the use of natural raw materials, may well mean that the design and form produced are of a higher standard than that produced by more sophisticated methods.

Tools and equipment

Man created the tools as well as the product of the tools and many of these have not changed in shape or function since virtually pre-history.

These tools need not be many or complex. Most primitive craftsmen in the past and indeed even today use only a small number of tools thus showing that a vast number of expensive gadgets are not necessary, or indeed desirable, as they tend to confuse rather than to help the beginner.

It is possible to begin with nothing more than a nail file and a pair of side cutting pliers (4) and only to graduate to more equipment when the need for it is felt. However, it would be silly to struggle along hampered by the lack of suitable tools and therefore there follows a list of tools which were useful in producing the work which is illustrated.

For working the metal
Small smooth-jawed bench vice
Tinman's snips, plumber's tinsnips, or jeweler's shears
Hand drill with bits
Hand files—flat, half round, round
Assorted needle files
Small hacksaw
Centre punch and scribe
Pliers with smooth jaws—round nose and flat nose
Lead block
Wood mallet
Wooden stakes or rods
Hammer

For soldering
Tweezers
Small brushes
Asbestos sheet
Solder (lead)
Lead solder flux
Gas torch or bunsen

tributing factor in deciding whether or not to attempt the craft with large numbers of students.

Some improvised tools and pieces of equipment are suggested within the appropriate sections and individuals may be able to create simple tools for particular jobs as the need arises.

For etching
Nitric acid
Ammonium sulphide
Glass dishes
Feathers
Paraffin wax

For polishing
Emery paper (various grades)
Soft cloth
Metal polish
Steel wool

Other aids, such as a large guillotine or bench shears for cutting metal, and such things as a polishing and buffing machine, are not necessary but would of course be useful if the craft was being conducted on a fairly large scale in schools or colleges. Many other tools of a more sophisticated nature can of course be used but the fact that these expensive pieces are not actually necessary is of importance to those who find that money is a con-

4 The minimum equipment: pliers with a side cutting edge and a nail file

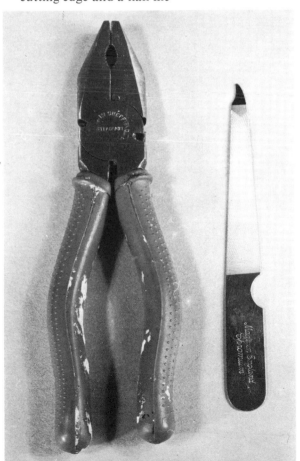

Work space

It is possible to produce jewelry in virtually any space large enough to hold a desk or table which is stable. If, in addition, it is located near light and water and is reasonably ventilated for soldering and heating operations so much the better.

Metal lacquer

Copper unfortunately tarnishes easily, but its surface can be protected by applying a colourless cellulose lacquer such as clear nail varnish or a lacquer produced for the purpose.

This, again unfortunately, detracts somewhat from the appearance of the metal and its use on decorative surfaces is not recommended. The copper article will acquire a more pleasant patina if worn unlacquered and it can be repolished at intervals if required.

However, it would be reasonable to use lacquer to protect the back of certain articles such as rings and pendants and this would also protect clothing from the effects of the tarnishing.

5   Some simple tools: hacksaw, tinman's snips,
     hammer, 4 files and a model maker's vice

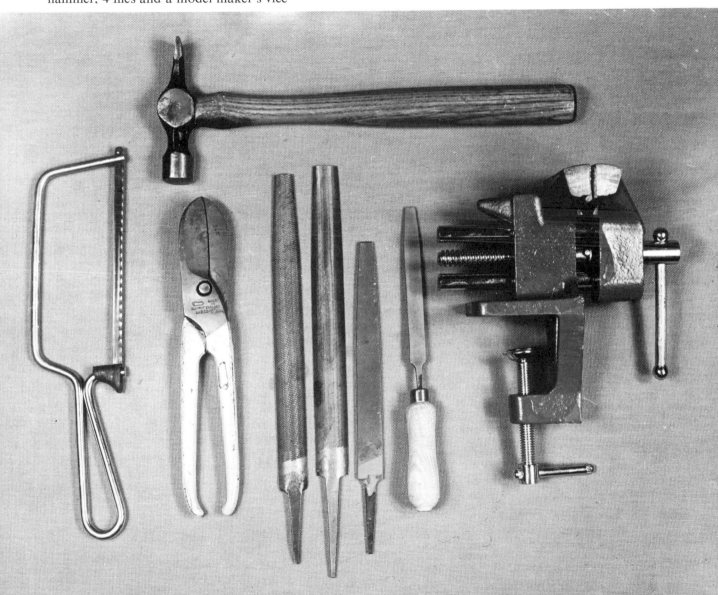

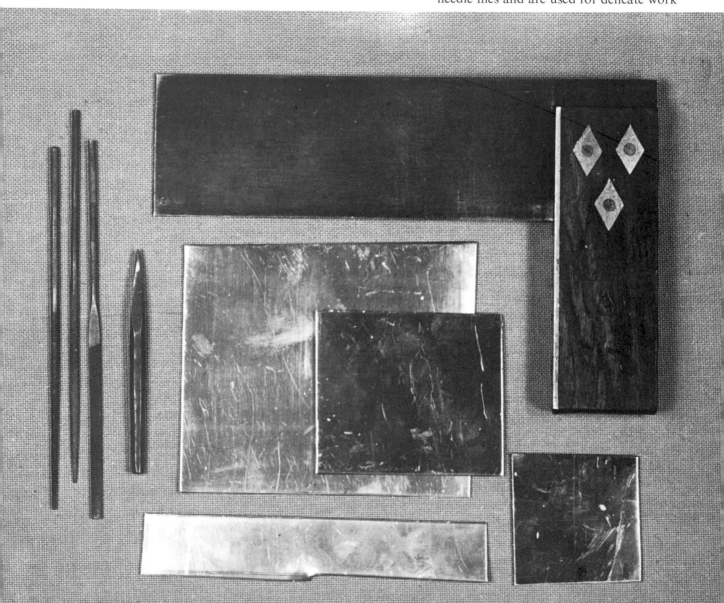

6 Copper sheet of various gauges with a try square and a steel punch that can act as a scriber. The three small files on the left are needle files and are used for delicate work

Design

Design, whether for jewelry or for any other
of the visual art forms, is based on the artist's
concern with shape, form, colour and surface
texture. The use of these things in conjunction
with each other can produce the particular
feeling that each individual designer is striving
to express.

It is not possible or desirable here to cover
in any detail the basic principles that are concerned in the creation of any single piece of
art work. However, the individual concerned
may already have some knowledge of design-
ing in another field using other materials and
of course this will be of immense value in the
creation of jewelry.

The majority of the examples shown are
based on traditional forms or are developed
from known historical examples and it is this
use of the museum that is suggested as a
sound basis for the beginner whether or not
he has had any training in basic design. In the
bibliography a number of books dealing with
design and form are listed. These do not
specifically mention jewelry but are suggested
as good background reading to any creative
design process in which the student may be
engaged.

Stimuli from natural forms

As well as the historical jewelry section of the museum, the natural history section may also be a rich source of ideas for visual forms. Indeed the close study of fern or bracken leaves uncurling or of the tendrils of sweet peas or convolvulus wrapping themselves round supports immediately suggest possibilities for wire forms. Drawings of these and of the vast number of possible stimuli lying around us can undoubtedly provide the starting point to innumerable designs of a highly inventive nature. The pieces of drift wood in figure 7 and the odd-shaped bones in figure 116 (section 6) are only two examples of the kind of 'found' object that can act as stimuli to the imagination in this way.

7   Three pieces of drift wood showing interest- ▶
ing form and pattern

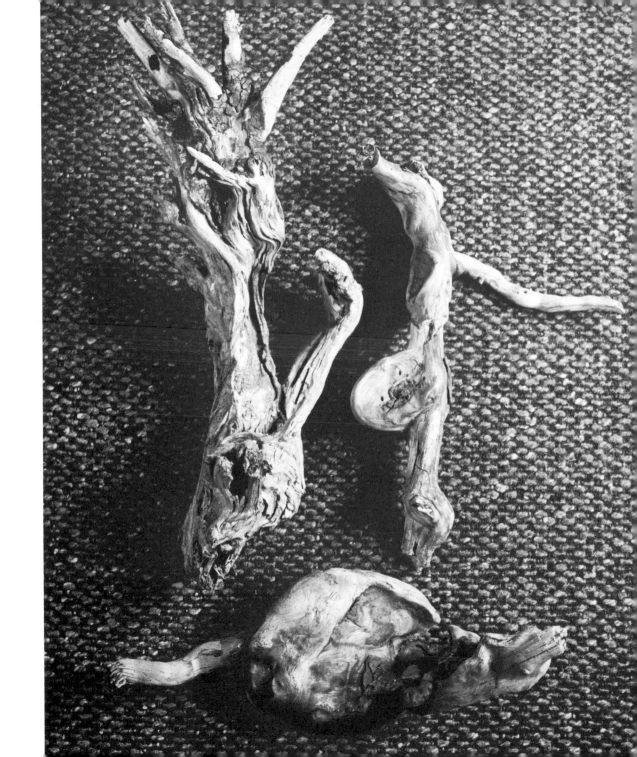

8 Necklace and brooches made by students from coiled copper wire. See also colour plate facing page 32

9 A gauge plate for measuring both wire and sheet metal

Section 2

Wire

While people generally think of wire as thin strip metal with a round section, the word means much more to a jeweler as he deals with wire in round, half-round, square, oval, or rectangular forms.

The making of odd sectioned wire involves the use of draw-plates or the purchasing of fairly expensive material, therefore the only wire used or referred to will be round sectioned wire that can be bought easily and cheaply.

In fact almost all the examples shown are made from ordinary soft copper wire that can be bought from most electricians, metal warehouses or hardware stores.

Wire, like sheet metal, is sold in various sizes called Imperial Standard Wire Gauge (UK) and Brown and Sharp (USA), and the most useful gauges are, 16, 18, and 20 gauge. (The smaller the gauge number the thicker the wire or sheet.)

The tools used to work wire can be as simple as an ordinary nail file and pair of side cutting pliers (4) and these are all that are necessary to produce quite complex pieces of work. If possible however two pairs of pliers should be obtained—a round-nosed pair and a flat-nosed pair—these should be smooth inside the jaws so that they do not mark the metal. If the only pliers available have toothed jaws a strip of sticking plaster over the teeth will help to protect the soft copper during working (10).

Wire is an extremely versatile material but like all substances it has its limitations and it is wise to respect these and not to attempt to torture it into shapes that do not suit it or come naturally to it. The following example is intended to give practise in working the wire and the illustrations of student work shown in figures 8, 11, 12, and 13, show the type of development that can follow once the basic techniques have been mastered.

Two pairs of round-nosed pliers and a pair of flat-nosed pliers with sticking plaster masking toothed jaws.

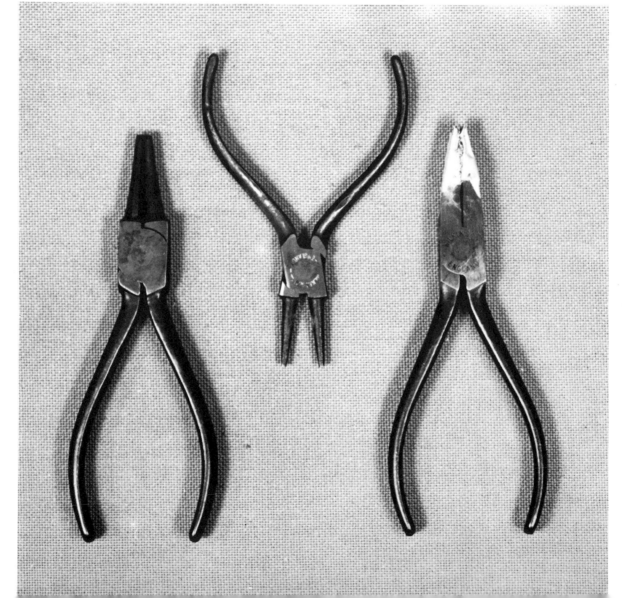

11 Examples of wire coiling by students

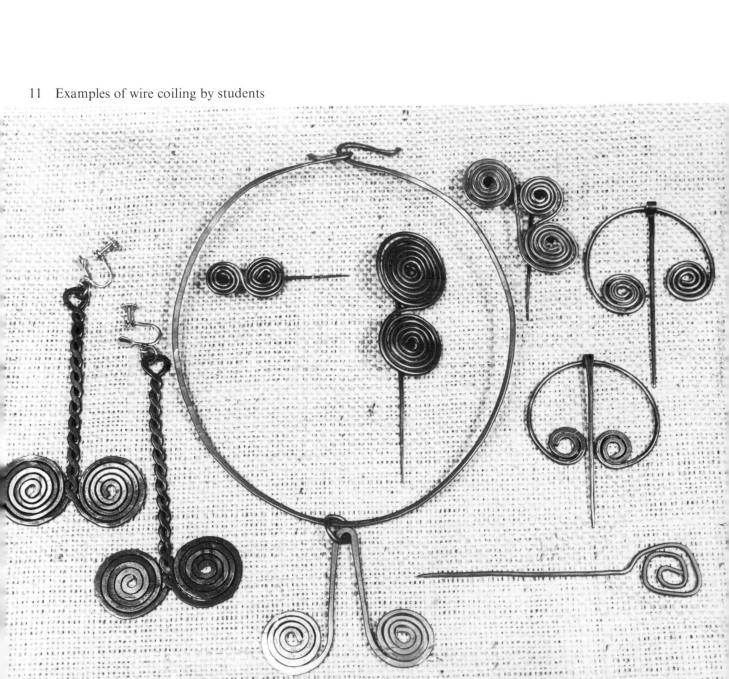

12 A coiled and hammered copper-wire brooch
made by a student

13 This coiled brooch was based on an early British example and has three tan-and-black enamelled pendants hanging from the enamelled central bars

14 Spectacle type Celtic fibula in bronze

15 Convex Disc: spiral coil of bronze wire. Found at Vulci in Italy and made in the fourth century B.C.

17 Bronze fibula brooch made about the fourth century B.C. on which the working example is based

The making of a 'facsimile'
Celtic brooch or pin

This is unfortunately an essentially non-creative exercise, in as much as the design is pre-determined, but serves as an ideal way of becoming familiar with the tools and equipment.

The following instructions set out as simply as possible the stages in construction of a pin similar to the one illustrated (see figure 17) which dates from about the fourth century B.C. and which was found at Capua in Italy.

Materials and equipment
This list gives the ideal equipment but there is no reason to suppose that the pin cannot be made with much less equipment as no doubt the original was produced with tools which were extremely primitive.

1 pair of round-nosed pliers
1 pair of flat-nosed pliers
1 pair of jeweler's or tinman's snips, plumber's tinsnips, or side cutting pliers
1 small vice
1 hammer
16- or 18-gauge soft copper wire
1 medium file
Polish and cloths
Emery paper
Nitric acid and ammonium sulphide.

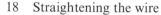

18   Straightening the wire

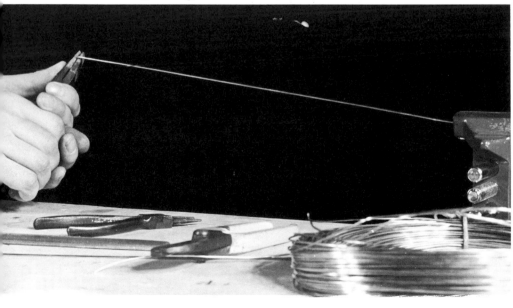

Stage 1 The wire should be cut to length—about 15 inches makes a reasonable-sized pin in 16-gauge wire—straightened and any kinks taken out. This is done by placing one end of the wire in the vice and taking hold of the other end with the flat pliers, making a sharp bend (see figure 18) and giving a few steady pulls to stretch the wire slightly.

When removed from the vice the ends of the wire, which may be slightly disfigured, can be cut off using the snips. At this stage the wire, now ready for use, should be treated carefully.

Stage 2 Holding the wire about four inches from one end in the flat-nosed pliers a right-angled bend is made by bending the wire firmly with the thumb against the sides of the pliers (19). The four-inch length will eventually become the sharp pin.

Stage 3 The coiling now begins and care should be taken here as a bad start tends to show all the way through the coiling. With the round-nosed pliers the wire is gripped as close to the right-angled bend as possible with the short end of wire lying the length of the pliers where it is held by the hand holding the pliers (20). The thumb of the other hand is then used to bend the wire tightly round the nose of the pliers, thus producing the first coil (20).

19   Making a right-angled bend

20   The first coil

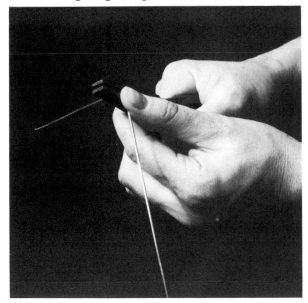

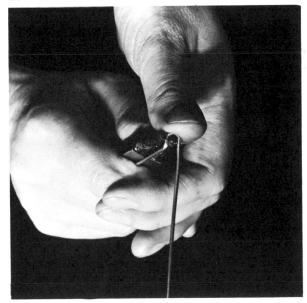

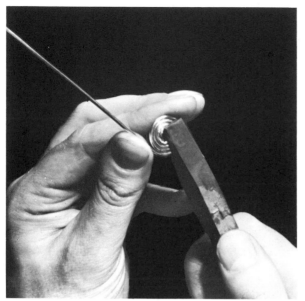

Stage 4 The round-nosed pliers are now discarded and with the flat-nosed pliers coiling continues, care being taken to coil as closely as possible and to keep the coiled area flat (21). If by any chance an error is made it is better to start with fresh wire than to vainly attempt to rectify odd bends in the wire.

This coiling continues until nearly half the length of wire is used.

Stage 5 The other end of the wire is now coiled in the opposite direction. (To produce an S-shaped brooch as in figure 17). The end should be filed smooth or rubbed on emery paper first and with the round-nosed pliers gripping as close to the end as possible, coiling is started (22). As soon as a start is made the pliers are changed for flat ones and coiling continues as before until the coils come together (23). At this stage it should be mentioned that for aesthetic reasons it is as well to have one coil slightly larger than the other.

21 Continuing the coiling

22 Starting the second coil

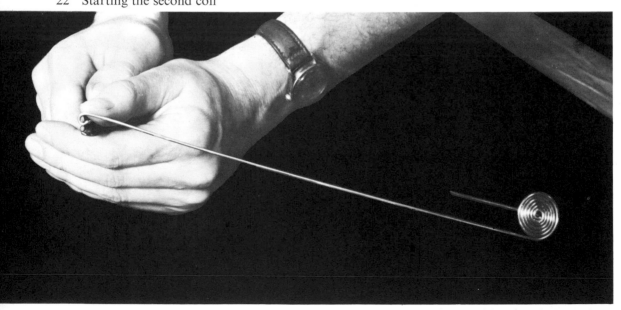

Copper-wire necklace and brooches made by ▶
college of education students

23 Completing the second coil

24 Sharpening the pin

Stage 6 It is now necessary to sharpen the pin and this is best done by laying the four inch length of wire along the head of the vice or any other similar place such as the edge of a block of wood (24). Using a medium file, held at an angle of 45 degrees the pin is sharpened by pushing towards the point. If turned round every now and again the pin can be given a tapered point which only needs rubbing on fine emery paper to give it a reasonable finish. At this stage a few taps with a hammer, using the flat of the hammer only, will help to toughen the metal of the pin (25).

The brooch is now gripped immediately behind the coils with the round-nosed pliers about halfway along the nose of the pliers and with the thumb, the pin is bent down the length of the coils until it just touches the lower coil (26). This completes the working and it is now only necessary to colour and polish the brooch.

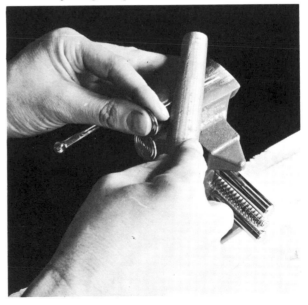

25 Hardening the pin

26 Bending the pin into its final position

27   The finished brooch

Stage 7 The completed brooch is now cleaned in a solution of nitric acid to remove all the dirt and grease which will have accumulated during the working (see section 3—Etching). After removal from the acid and washing in clean water, a dip in ammonium sulphide solution for a few seconds will completely blacken the brooch. After drying, the brooch can be polished by hand by rubbing against a cloth which has a few drops of metal polish on it. This method of rubbing against a pad of cloth is much more satisfactory than holding both cloth and brooch by hand.

The polishing will not remove the blackening from between the coils and the result will give the finished brooch a reasonably pleasant antique appearance which will improve with age.

28 Wooden stakes and a boxwood mallet

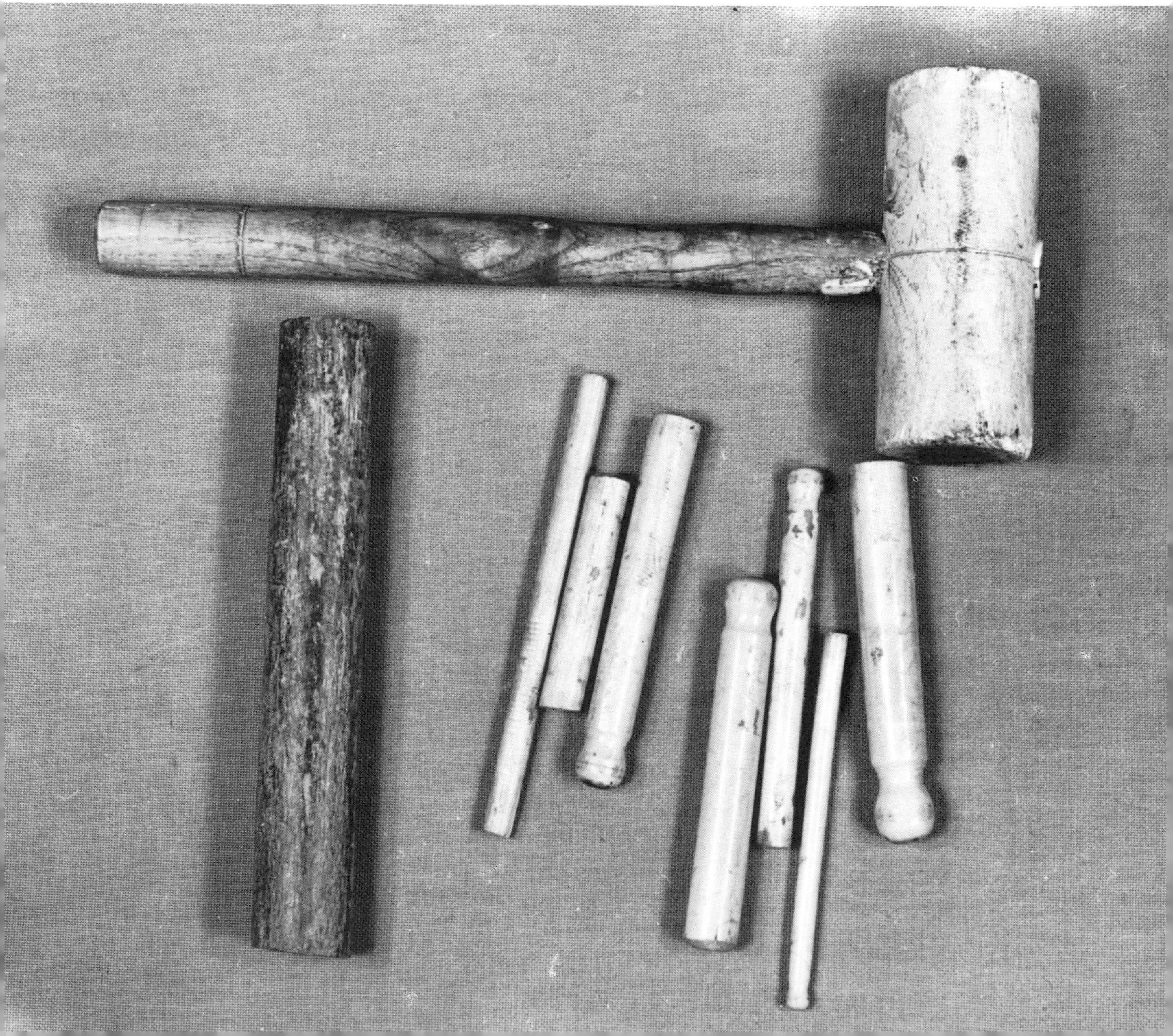

Wire links and chain

One of the most obvious uses for wire is in chain making, and this is very easily done in the following manner.

To make numerous links of the same size and shape, a former of some kind must be used. Here various things such as wooden dowelling or knitting needles of various sizes are ideal (28).

Stage 1 The wire should be prepared and the former placed in the vice which should also hold one end of the wire.

Stage 2 The wire is now wound round the former by hand as tightly and evenly as possible. Each turn will produce a link (29).

29   Winding soft wire round the stake

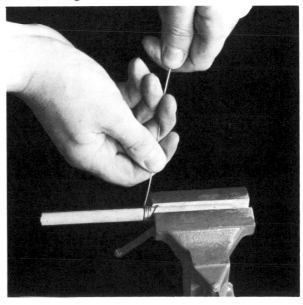

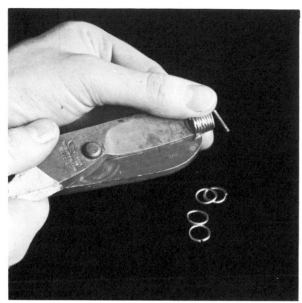

30　Cutting the links with snips

Stage 3 The coils can now be sawn through if a jeweler's saw is available or cut with the snips as in figure 30.

Stage 4 Any roughness at the cuts should be cleaned with a file or emery paper and the links closed up. Ideally each link should be soldered but quite strong chain can be produced without soldering and links for pendants, etc. do not usually require to be soldered.

31　Cut links with a portion of uncut coil on the left. The open misshapen link in the foreground shows the wrong method of opening links while the link opened sideways in the pliers shows the correct method

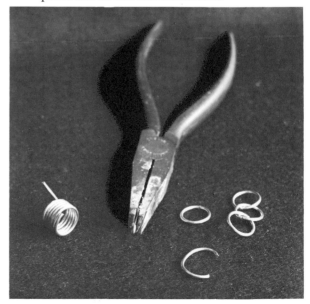

32 (a) Finger ring in bronze wire similar to the working example. Celtic third or fourth century B.C.

(b) Finger ring in gold from the same period

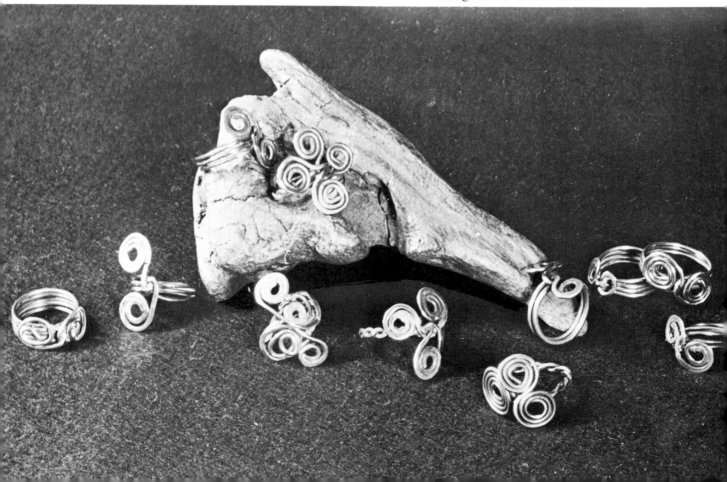

33 Selection of copper-wire rings made by college of education students

34　Bending and crossing the wire on the wooden stake

35　Adjusting the length of the wire before coiling

A wire ring

The following method of producing a ring is merely shown as a basic idea and, as can be seen from the selection in figure 33, many variations can be made on this basic form.

Materials and equipment
As well as the usual equipment for working with wire a number of wooden stakes are necessary. These stakes can be dowelling or other suitable round wooden rods (28) which are the same circumference as the fingers for which the rings are being made.

Stage 1 A length of 16- or 18-gauge wire—about 8 or 9 inches is ample—is straightened and prepared as usual and then a suitably-sized wooden stake is placed in the vice.

The wire is bent round the stake (34) either twice or three times according to preference. The ends of the wire are then crossed as this stabilizes the whole ring and makes any movement in the coils unlikely.

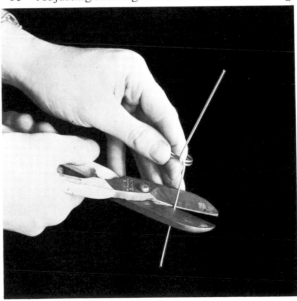

Stage 2 The ends of the wire are now cut to suitable lengths (35) and can now be coiled or bent into some decorative shape using the pliers as in the previous example (36).

Stage 3 A hammer is used to flatten and strengthen the decorative coils. The ring is placed in the vice with the coils lying on the head of the vice. Using the hammer carefully and only striking with the flat of the head and never with the edge, as this could sever the wire, the coils are flattened and spread to enhance the design (37).

Stage 4 The ring is now rubbed with emery paper to remove any scratches or marks and this is often better done by holding the ring and rubbing against a sheet of emery which is placed on a firm surface. Cleaning with a solution of nitric acid follows and blackening with ammonium sulphide. A final polish with metal polish and a soft cloth produces the finished ring (38).

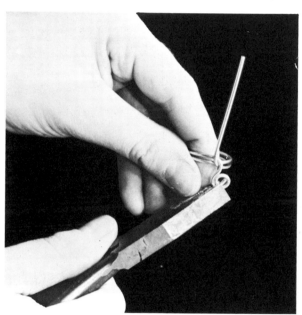

36 Producing the decorative coiling

37 Hammering the decorative coils

38 The finished ring

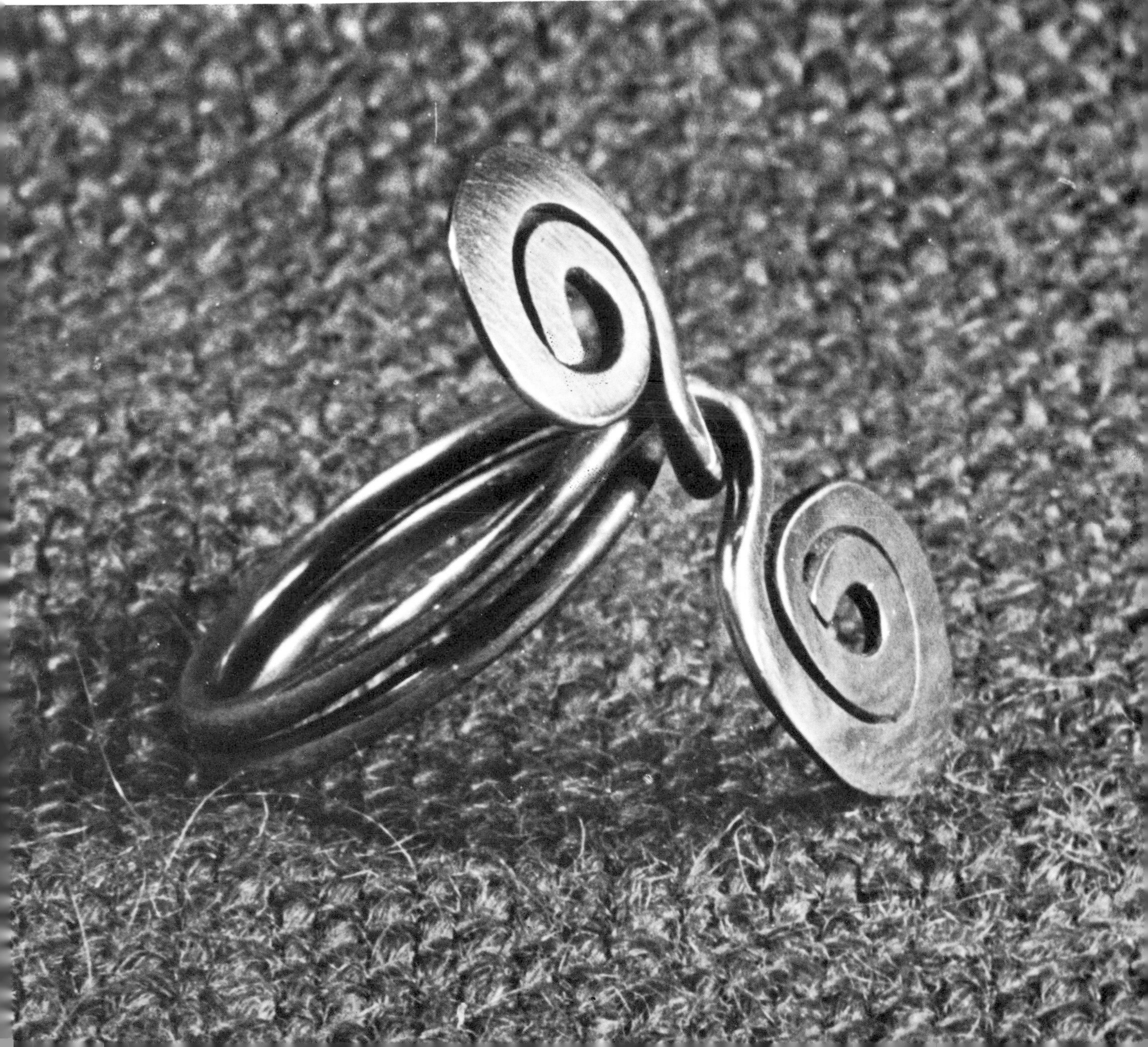

Annealing

One characteristic of metals which must be mentioned is 'work-hardening'.

Various stresses are created during the bending, hammering, twisting and shaping processes which result in a hardening of the metal. This is known as 'work-hardening' and can eventually lead to the metal actually fracturing.

To counteract this hardening the metal must be 'annealed'. This is done by heating to a certain temperature and then cooling quickly or slowly according to the metal and this relieves the stresses and restores the workability.

Copper is annealed by heating uniformly to a dull red colour and quenching in water, after which the oxides formed on the surface can be removed by dipping in weak acid.

Work hardening can of course be a useful method of strengthening things such as brooch pins and in the wire brooch example this is used to advantage.

39 Twisted, hammered and bound copper-wire
bracelets made by students

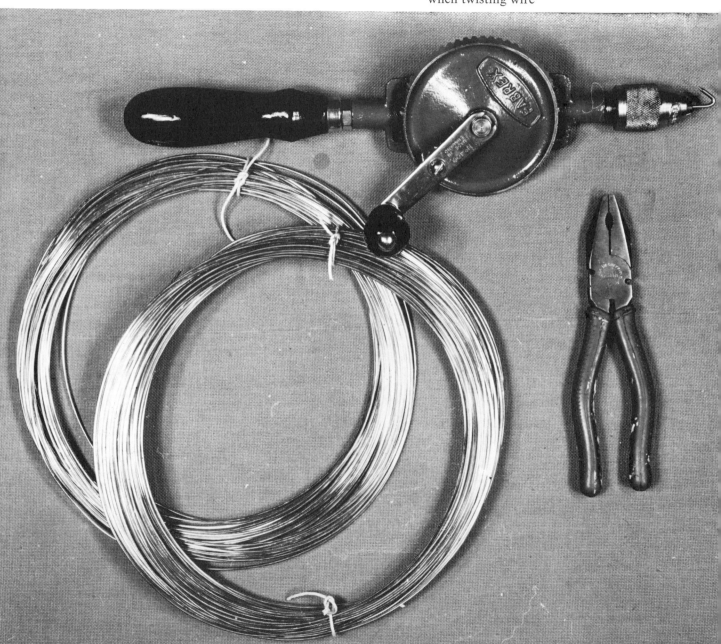

40 Coils of copper wire with a pair of side cutting pliers and a twist drill. The drill has a bent nail in the chuck as a hook for use when twisting wire

Twisting and hammering

Wire can very easily be twisted into extremely decorative lengths which can then be used to produce articles which require more decoration than plain wire can provide. Some of the rings in figure 33 have been made from wire which has been twisted for part of its length and twisted and flattened wire was used to produce the bracelets in figure 39 and 41. There is no reason either why wire treated in this way cannot be soldered onto other articles as required.

The tools required are merely the vice and a pair of square-nosed pliers but a hand drill ensures a much more regular effect.

The wire which should be soft, i.e. annealed is folded in half and the two ends placed together in the vice while the other end is hooked with a cup hook or bent nail which is in the chuck of the drill (42).

The possible variations are so numerous that some time can be spent profitably on experiments with various gauges of wire, and it might be wise to keep a record of the results and how they were obtained.

41 A wire bracelet made from a flattened twist and two single flattened wires
42 Twisting wire using a hand drill

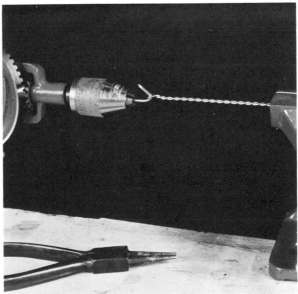

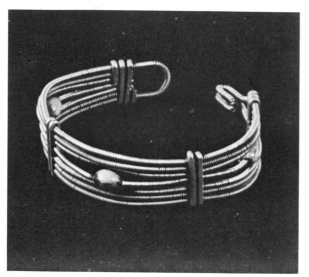

This twisted wire can now, if desired, be hammered flat, thus producing yet another effect that can be usefully employed in certain articles. Indeed any wire can be flattened by hammering to change its character often with advantage as in the wire ring in figure 38 or the bracelets in figures 39 and 41.

Hammering is done with a flat hammer and the wire is held against a steel block or as in this case the little anvil on the vice. The flat of the hammer only is used as a blow from the edge could sever the wire. Steady, regular blows should be used rather than heavy ones and the wire may have to be annealed at intervals although this is often unnecessary.

Wire bracelets

The wire bracelets in figures 39 and 41 were constructed from twisted and hammered wires which were bound together with finer wire, hammered lightly again to consolidate the binding and then shaped around wooden stakes in exactly the same way as the rings on page 40.

43   A copy of an African bracelet made from galvanised wire bound in soft 22-gauge copper wire and with hard seeds threaded as decoration. The strands are held together by being bound with heavy gauge wire hammered into position

44   A breakdown of the construction of the wire necklace shown in figure 8. The lengths of 16- or 18-gauge wire each measure 10 inches

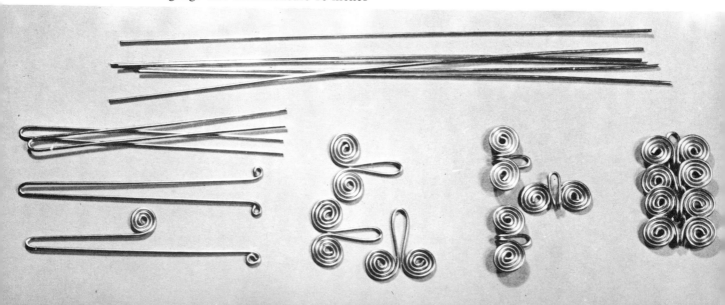

45 An etched pendant made from 18-gauge sheet copper

Section 3

Etching

The illustration in figure 46 shows a Pictish silver ornament with a design which was probably cut into the silver using a harder metal tool of some sort, i.e. engraved. A similar effect can be achieved more easily by using acid to do the hard work of cutting the metal. The instructions that follow set out as simply as possible the stages in construction of a simple copper pendant with an etched decoration. The design chosen depends on various factors but generally it is wise to start with a fairly simple pattern and to avoid difficult linear drawing.

Materials and equipment
1 pair of jeweler's or tinman's snips
1 small vice
1 medium file
1 hammer
1 wooden mallet
Nitric acid
Ammonium sulphide
2 or 3 glass dishes
Feathers
Candle wax or paraffin wax and a tin or recepticle for melting it
Copper sheet 18 or 16 gauge.

46 Silver plaque with Pictish symbols such as are found on carved stone monuments. From the hoard of silver ornaments found at Norrie's Law, Largo, Fife (seventh to eighth century A.D.)

Stage 1 A suitable piece of copper is cut from the sheet—18 gauge was used in this case. This is done by 'scribing' the lines on the sheet using a square or steel ruler and a sharp needle scriber or the end of a suitable file (47).

The snips are then used to cut the sheets (48) and care should be taken to cut without ever actually finishing the cuts with the snips as this can cause a very ragged edge.

When the shape has been cut it is usually necessary to flatten it using a wooden flat headed mallet and working against a wooden surface (49). This saves any unnecessary marking of the copper. If however the bending of the corners proves stubborn it may be

47 Scribing lines on sheet copper

48 Cutting the sheet with tinman's snips

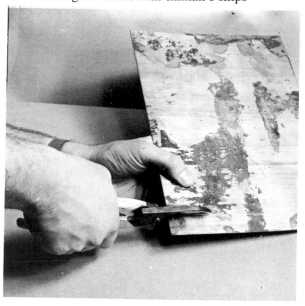

necessary to tap these out with a metal hammer against a metal surface, i.e. the anvil, which is provided on most small vices.

Stage 2 The edges of the piece must now be filed and cleaned and this is done by placing it in the vice so that only one edge protrudes about a quarter of an inch. The file is used at an angle of roughly 45 degrees to the edge and pushed or drawn on the edge until a flat surface is produced (50). This is repeated on all sides and the corners are softened to remove any sharp edges. Emery paper is next used on the sides and surface of the piece until a good finish is acquired.

49　Removing dents with a wooden mallet

50　Filing the edge

Stage 3 At this point a hole for either a thong or ring should be drilled or punched. This should be done by marking with a hand punch and hammer (51) and then either punching out using a punch as illustrated (52) or drilling with a hand drill while the piece is held in the vice.

Stage 4 The pendant is now coated with 'wax' (53). A candle or some paraffin wax is melted in a suitable container—a coffee tin is ideal—and when it is just smoking the wax is brushed

51   Marking with a steel punch

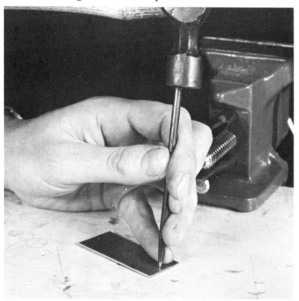

52   Punching a hole

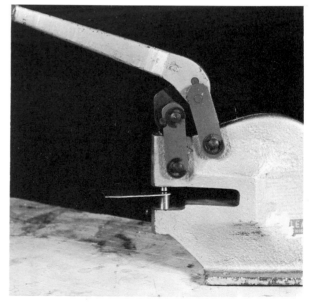

on to the surface of the copper. The piece is held over the tin of molten wax and the loaded brush is quickly brushed down half the surface allowing any residue to fall back into the tin (54). The piece is turned round and all surfaces are brushed with the wax until a reasonable thickness is achieved. The wax, if too thick, will crack during the cutting of the design and if too thin difficulty will be experienced in scratching it out of some areas. About four brushed layers are usually enough to give a working surface.

53 Container with brushes, paraffin wax and candles

54 Brushing on the wax

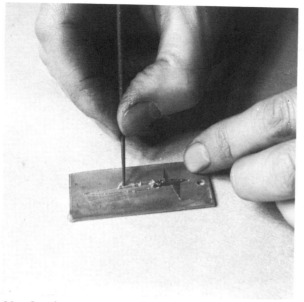

55 Cutting the design through the wax

56 Etching in nitric-acid solution

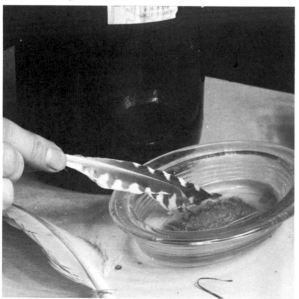

Stage 5 It is now necessary to cut away the wax from those areas that are to be attacked by the acid. This is done using an etching needle or any instrument that is sharp and can be held comfortably.

The wax should be cut through carefully in order to avoid cracking and lifting the wax from the surface of the copper and the sides of the cuts should slope inwards as do those of a canal (55). Any undercutting may result in the wax lifting during the actual etching of the acid. When the design has been completely cut the piece should be checked carefully and any inadvertantly exposed areas of copper must be covered with more wax. The edges and the area of the punched hole are the most likely places to have lost wax during the cutting process.

Stage 6 The acid bath is prepared by making a solution of one part nitric acid to three parts water. For safety the acid should be added to the water and the fumes should under no circumstances be inhaled. This work is best carried out in a well ventilated area and glass containers should always be used.

The etching bath can be used until it turns dark blue and need only be discarded when this happens. It should be stored in a tightly-stoppered bottle and when eventually discarded it must be washed down the drain with plenty of running water to avoid damage to the pipes.

The piece is now immersed in the acid bath (56) and the bubbles that appear are occasionally brushed away with a feather. If the etching is taking place too quickly the heat created could melt the wax, therefore if this appears to be the case it is as well to dilute the solution slightly by adding it to more water in another dish.

The depth of etch can be varied according to taste, and the piece can be removed and washed in clean water every now and again to check the process.

When the etching is complete, rinse the piece in cold water and then the wax is most easily removed by running it under a hot tap. This will remove the wax completely but care should be taken that no wax is allowed to clog the drains.

Stage 7 A solution of ammonium sulphide is now placed in a dish and the piece placed in it for a few moments (57). This produces a black colour over the entire surface of the copper.

Stage 8 The pendant is now polished by rubbing against a cloth with some drops of metal polish on it and the black will be removed fairly easily from the flat surfaces but will remain in the etched areas thus enhancing the design (58). A thong of leather or a suitable chain completes the pendant (59).

57 Blackening in ammonium sulphide

59 The finished pendant

58 Polishing against a pad of cloth

60 Expanding rings showing
etched decoration

An etched ring

The expanding rings in figure 60 were etched
in exactly the same manner as the pendant in
the previous example. The sheet metal, in this
case 20 gauge, was cut into a strip of suitable
width and to a length suitable for the finger.
This should be a little less than the circumference of the finger which can be measured
easily by winding soft wire or string around
the finger, cutting the wire or string and
straightening it out to give the correct measure-
ment.

The corners of the strip can be snipped off
and the ends curved to give them an attractive
finish, after which the edges and surface are
cleaned prior to coating with wax. Care should
be taken not to use a design which will produce
weakness across the width of the ring as this
may give rise to difficulties when the ring is
beaten into shape.

After etching, the flat piece of copper has to
be beaten round a stake which should be
slightly smaller than the finished size for the
ring. The handle of a wooden spoon or any
suitable piece of dowelling can be used. A flat-
headed wooden mallet is used (28) and as the
ring is held at right angles to the stake, the
blows from the mallet gradually curve it
round the stake until the complete circle is
achieved.

The finished ring is coloured and lacquered
on the inside to prevent discolouration of the
finger.

61 Etched pendants with the right-hand example showing etching of different depths. This would be achieved by stopping out the lower area after a few minutes and allowing the upper area to be etched for a longer period

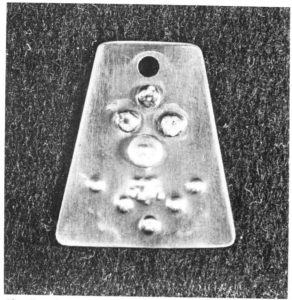

62   Pendant with hammered decoration combined with decorative soldered studs

Hammering

Hammering is not a jeweler's term but the techniques of engraving, matting, repousse and chasing involve buying tools that perhaps would be rather expensive.

To produce effects similar to these techniques is possible, however, by using simply a hammer and a few odd-shaped large nails and other odds and ends.

The small pendant in figure 62 was formed from a piece of sheet copper that had been laid on a lead block (a soft wooden surface would also be suitable) and marked with an ordinary nail which was hammered on the surface to produce dents of various depths. Either side can then be used to give concave or convex effects. The pendant was completed by soldering on circles of copper which were left after punching holes in another sheet, discolouring and finally polishing.

Surface texture can be produced by hammering dust into the polished surface of articles or by laying wire mesh on the sheet metal and hammering it in, to produce a mesh pattern. The pendant in figure 71 shows the use of textured surfaces which were produced with a hammer and a nail. The possibilities in this field are unlimited and work of this type is so simple that it can be used even with very young children.

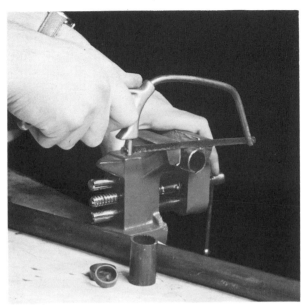

63   Cutting the pipe to produce a ring

64   Filing the edges of the ring

Rings from copper pipe

This method of producing rings is both simple and obvious. Suitable pipe is obtained by merely trying various sizes until one is found that fits the chosen finger. A small section is then cut to produce the ring.

Stage 1 Having chosen the pipe, place it in the vice a little below the top surface and parallel to it with the portion to be cut protruding from one end.
   A sharp hacksaw is now used to cut this section and the edge of the vice is used as a guide to the blade. This keeps the blade steady and makes it possible to cut in a straight line (63).

Stage 2 The ring has now only to be cleaned, using a file for the rough edges as in figure 64. Rubbing thus against the file gives greater control and more pressure if required.

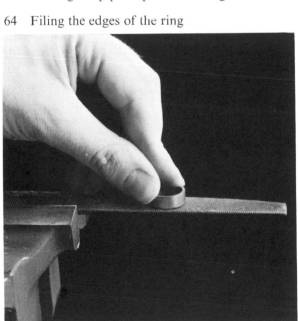

65 Cleaning with emery paper

Stage 3 Emery can now be used to remove any scratches and the sharp edges should be smoothed by wrapping a little emery around a finger and working on the inside of the ring (65).

Stage 4 A final polish against some cloth with metal polish on it will give a good finish (66). The ring could of course be decorated by soldering other metal forms to it or by filing some decorative pattern on the surface.

The ring in figure 67 is made from copper pipe and the filed groove round the centre filled with black enamel.

66 Polishing against a pad of cloth

67 A finger ring made from copper pipe with a
filed groove filled with black enamel

68 A pendant made by a student using hammered wire and soldering techniques

69 A pendant made by soldering bent wire on to a filed base plate

Section 4

Soldering

One of the easiest methods of joining two pieces of metal is by soldering them together and as lead solder is cheaper and melts at a very low temperature it is more practical to use than other solders that require higher temperatures and more equipment. Indeed very little in the way of equipment is necessary, as a bunsen burner or small gas torch can be used as a source of heat and the only other essential article is a sheet of soft fibrous asbestos on which to work. An inexpensive propane gas torch is now on the market as well. A pair of tweezers would also be useful and anything suitable such as eye-brow tweezers can be used.

The method of soldering described in the following example is usually referred to as 'sweat soldering' and does not involve the use of a soldering iron.

The examples made by students in figures 68, 69, 70 and 71 all involve the use of soldering and it can be seen that other techniques such as etching are used, and in some cases the surface of the metal has been hammered to produce a decorative effect.

70 Earrings made from 20-gauge copper with bars of the same gauge metal soldered across the lower half

71 This pendant made from sheet metal and hammered wire also shows the use of hammered dents as textural decoration

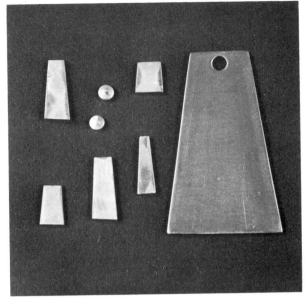

72 All the assembled parts are 18-gauge copper sheet except the studs which are 18-gauge nickel silver

A soldered pendant

This example serves to illustrate the technique of sweat soldering . A number of pieces of metal are attached to a base piece to produce a decorative pendant.

Materials and equipment

As well as the usual tools used to work copper the following are necessary.
1 gas torch or bunsen burner
1 soft asbestos sheet
Tweezers
Lead solder
Flux.

Stage 1 The copper pieces which are to form the pendant are shaped and thoroughly cleaned and all the edges are finished as it is extremely difficult to reach some areas after assembly. Any holes should be punched and generally a good finish given to all the component parts (72).

Stage 2 The base piece should be laid on the asbestos sheet and some flux applied to the areas that will be underneath the decorative pieces. The solder which must be cut into very small pieces (73) should be placed in

73 Cutting the solder into small pieces

74 Positioning the solder

position on the base piece, using the tweezers (74). The decorative pieces to be attached are brushed with flux on the underside and placed in position on top of the pieces of solder. Flux is necessary to slow up the process of oxidisation which takes place when the metal is heated and by doing this and keeping the surfaces clean it allows the solder to flow properly.

Stage 3 The gas torch is now lit and the heat applied gently to the large base piece of metal taking care that any bubbling of the flux does not move any of the smaller pieces.

The small pieces of metal will fall into place as the solder beneath them melts and the flame can then be played more generally over the entire piece to spread the solder (75). Very little solder should be used and therefore

75 Applying the heat

76 Cleaning in a solution of nitric acid

there should be no danger of the solder spreading on to the other parts of the base piece.

Alternatively it is possible to melt solder on to the back of the small pieces and then add more flux and place them in position on the base piece. Then, in a second operation, heat until the parts are soldered together.

Stage 4 The piece is now allowed to cool and washed in hot water to remove any excess flux. It can then be cleaned in nitric acid (76), washed again, dried and polished with emery and metal polish or fine wire wool as in figure 77.

Stage 5 A dip in ammonium sulphide (78) will blacken the entire work and it can be finished by polishing with metal polish and a soft cloth (79).

77   Polishing with steel wool

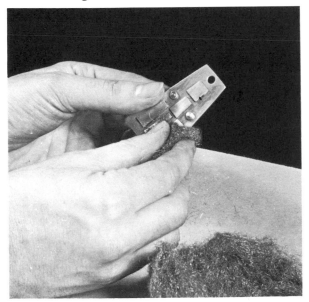

78   Blackening with ammonium sulphide

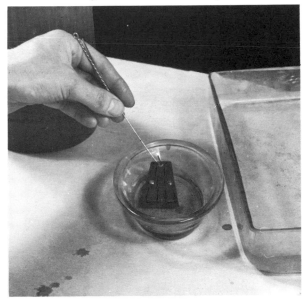

79   The finished pendant

81 Two brooches and two pendants made from fused masses of scrap copper soldered to base plates. In the pendants etched decoration has also been used

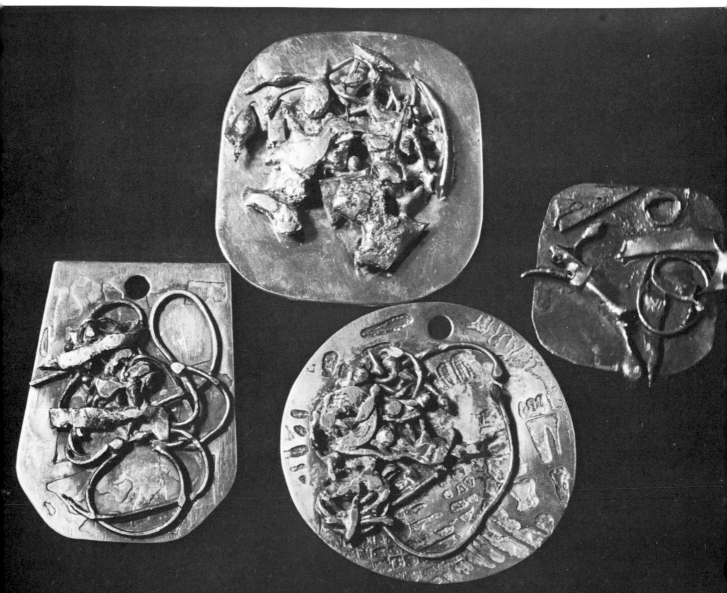

82 The gas torch being used to fuse copper scraps on an asbestos sheet

83 Two brooches and a pendant made by fusing scraps of silver

Melting and fusing

If a flame is played on the surface of a sheet of metal it will gradually melt first the surface and then the entire piece. If the flame is removed at the critical moment it is possible to melt just the surface giving a molten looking appearance which, although impossible to control exactly, can be extremely decorative. illustrated catalogue to help selection.

Likewise, if small scrap pieces of metal are arranged on the surface they will partially melt and fuse to the surface producing even heavier texturing.

The examples shown in figure 81 were produced by fusing scrap copper wire and off-cuts of sheet copper and then soldering these masses on to a back plate of polished sheet copper or in one case sheet nickel silver.

The work must be done on an asbestos sheet and if the scraps are raised slightly, say on two large nails there is less chance of loss of heat and fusion will be achieved very quickly (82).

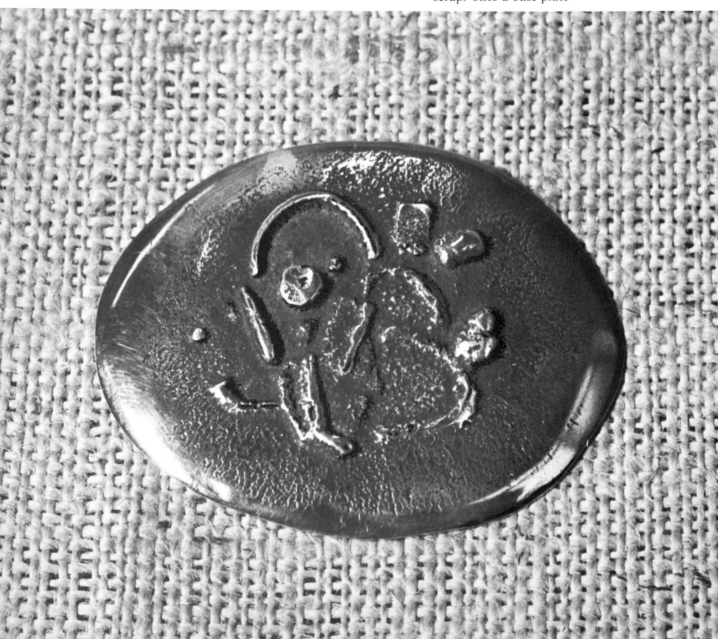

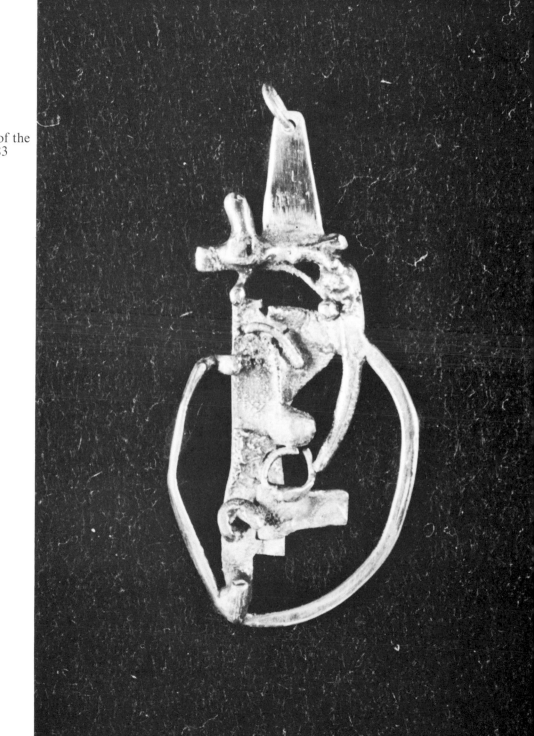

85 An enlarged view of the pendant in figure 83

Section 5

Findings

Jeweler's findings are those small items such as ear clips, catches, pins, etc. which can be bought ready-made for use, in jeweler's suppliers.

Their use saves time and effort in the production of individual fittings and in the case of earrings at least, they are almost necessary, as gold or silver are the only metals suitable for contact with pierced ears.

These fittings are soldered on to the piece of finished jewelry in the usual way or they can be glued in position using Araldite or some other strong adhesive.

Findings can often be purchased from local jewelers but usually it is best to buy them from wholesale suppliers who would supply an illustrated catalogue to help selection.

It is of course possible to make most catches and hooks. The illustrations of work show a number of methods of linking and joining items. Figure 87 shows a simple hook and ring made from two gauges of copper wire, fastened to the leather thong which has been cut to the exact size required.

Enamelling

The art of enamelling dates back at least 2000 years and enamelled jewelry is still popular for the brilliance and variety of its colours. Figure 86 shows some examples of enamelling from southern Scotland made about A.D. 100.

Enamel is a kind of glass, ground to powder, and fused with heat on a metal surface as a vitreous glaze which is coloured by the metal oxides present in the enamels.

Copper, silver, gold, and steel are the metals most commonly used with enamel and generally silver gives the best results as it gives a great degree of reflection through the translucent or transparent enamels. Enamel can also be opaque and a great variety of brilliant colours can be purchased either in powder or lump form (88).

There are five main techniques for applying enamels. They are Limoges, Cloisonné, Champlevé, Baisse-taille, and Plique-à-jour. Of these the Limoges method is the most suitable for the beginner and is therefore the method used in the working example which follows. It is usually supposed that enamelling is a difficult

86 Enamelled bronze brooches
Left Dragonesque brooch in red and blue.
Northern Romano British, A.D. 100. From
Lamberton Moor, Berwickshire
Centre Red, gray and white enamelled brooch
from Camelon Fort near Falkirk
Right Dragonesque brooch from Newstead,
Melrose

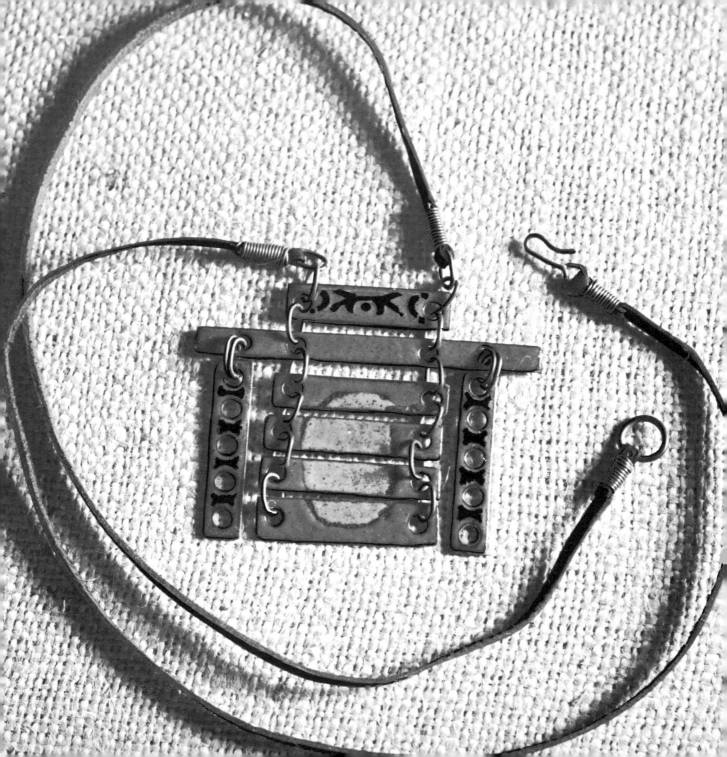

process that involves high temperatures and quantities of expensive equipment, but this is not necessarily the case.

It is possible to produce perfectly good enamelled pieces for jewelry purposes with nothing more elaborate in the way of a kiln than a bunsen burner or a gas torch and it is even possible to fire pieces on an ordinary gas or electric kitchen cooker.

The method then is to pound or grind the lumps of enamel into powder using a mortar and pestle (89) and to wash the resulting powder until no impurities remain. This is done by placing the enamel powder in a glass jar and filling it up with clean water, pausing for a moment to allow the enamel to fall to the bottom of the jar and then pouring off the milky water. This is repeated a few times until the water remains clear.

The powder is now dried in a dish in the oven

87 Strips of enameled copper joined with copper-wire links to produce a pendant which is completed by the addition of a leather thong and simple catch

88 Jars of powdered enamel with some lump enamel in the foreground

89 Mortar and pestle

90 Method of firing on wire mesh or expanded
    metal

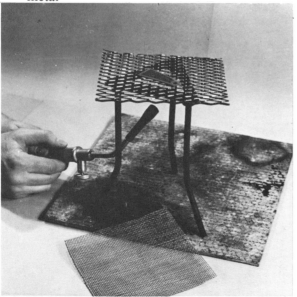

or spread out on some suitable surface and dried over a low bunsen flame and then stored in a small jar or bottle (88).

As well as enamels it is necessary to have a kiln of some kind and although ideally a good commercial kiln is best it is possible to enamel with nothing more elaborate than a tripod stand and a bunsen burner or gas torch. The pieces for firing are placed on wire mesh or expanded metal on top of the tripod (90) and the heat applied from below. It is possible to fire from above by playing the flame directly on to the surface of the enamel but this is likely to discolour the enamel and produce chance effects, therefore it is not to be recommended. Likewise it is possible that the edges of the enamel pieces may be discoloured even through the wire mesh and it is sometimes

Enamel pieces in a variety of blues made by college ▶
of education students

91 Constructing shaker boxes from fine wire
    mesh

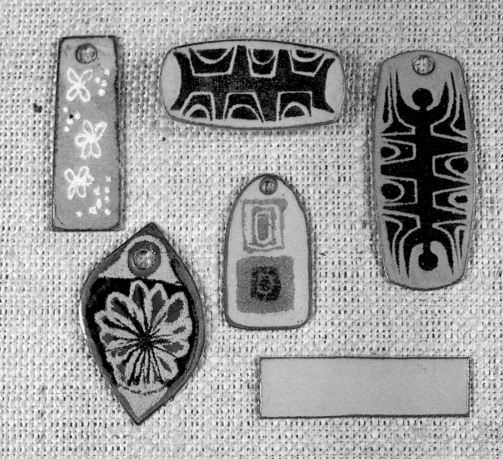

helpful to build a sort of hammock out of sheet nickel which gives complete protection from the flame (95). As always a fair amount of heat is generated, so it is wise to stand all these on an asbestos sheet or a couple of fire bricks.

The only other articles of equipment which are necessary are, shaker boxes or sieves made from wire mesh of 80 or 60 mesh (91), but even these can be made very cheaply by using trays from match boxes removing the bottom and replacing it with small sheets of cotton organdie glued round the sides. Small glass jars could be used with the opening covered with a piece of nylon stocking.

A spatula or palette knife is very useful for placing pieces in, and removing pieces from the kiln but an old kitchen knife will do just as well.

Copper is a first-class metal for enamelling as it is cheap, does not melt at enamelling temperatures which are usually about 700–800 degrees Centigrade (1300–1400 degrees Fahrenheit), and stands up to rough treatment.

Cleanliness is vital in enamelling and care must be taken at all times to keep the enamel powders clean. With this in mind it is wise to keep all other processes, such as filing, shaping, soldering, etc. at some distance from the enamelling area and introduce a fairly organised system of working especially if a number of different people are using the same enamels and tools.

The working example that follows shows one of the simplest methods of working and, as will be seen, there are no expensive tools or pieces of equipment involved.

Page 81

92   A pendant and two brooches in coloured enamels

93   Dusting the surface with enamel powder

Enamelling a simple pendant

The following example shows the Limoges process of enamelling where the entire surface area of the metal is covered with enamel. Nothing divides the areas of enamel from each other as in Cloisonné or other methods. The enamels can be applied by dusting, painting, or stenciling and it is possible to introduce glass beads or chunks of enamel to vary the surface. In the example, however, a simple two colour design has been chosen to show clearly the processes involved.

Materials and equipment
Copper sheet 18 gauge
Enamels in powder form
80-mesh wire screen folded into shaker boxes
Spatula or palette knife
Sheets of paper
Light machine oil or glycerine
Brushes and pens.

Stage 1 The simplest method is to dust the enamel on to the clean copper sheet which has already been shaped and prepared. To make certain that the powdered enamel sticks to the surface, the copper can have a coat of gum arabic solution painted on the surface but with most flat objects this should not be necessary.

The first stage then is to prepare the copper piece and to ensure that it is thoroughly clean. It would be as well to pass it through a solution of nitric acid, after which it must be washed and dried carefully and handled only by the edges.

Stage 2 Lay the prepared piece on a clean piece of smooth paper with perhaps a coin to prop it up at one corner so that the spatula can be inserted underneath it.

The powdered enamel is now placed in a wire-mesh box shaker and applied by dusting over the whole surface. This is done by holding the shaker about two or three inches above the piece and tapping it with the forefinger or by gently shaking it to and fro. The aim is to achieve an even covering of enamel (93).

Stage 3 The spatula is now used to lift the sprinkled piece (94) and place it in the kiln (95). The excess enamel on the sheet of paper should now be replaced in the container (96).

Stage 4 The bunsen or bunsens (or gas torch) are now lit and turned fully on to achieve as much heat as possible and placed directly below the piece to be fired. The enamel will first appear to discolour slightly and then to glisten as it begins to melt and fuse to the surface of the copper.

When an even glassy appearance is evident the heat can be removed and the piece allowed to cool (97).

94 Lifting the piece

95 Placing in the kiln

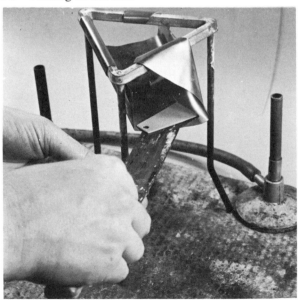

Stage 5 Having produced a piece with a simple colour over the entire surface, it is possible now to fire other colours in a decorative pattern on top of this.

If a drawing is made on the enamel surface using light machine oil and a pen or brush (98), it will be found that a second dusting with a contrasting colour of enamel will adhere to the oil drawing and any excess can be removed from the other areas by tapping the piece gently on the end (99) or by using a small brush.

During this second dusting it is important that no fire scale from the back of the piece becomes mixed with the enamel as this spoils it for future use. To avoid this possibility the back of the piece should be cleaned with emery between firings, or a saline solution can be applied to the back beforehand. This prevents fire scale from sticking and facilitates its removal. One tablespoon of salt to a cup of water makes a suitable solution that can be applied by brush.

When the second dusting has been completed the piece is returned to the kiln and refired. The second colour can be seen to melt and fuse with the first firing and the process is complete when an even glassy surface is achieved (100).

The piece is allowed to cool and then the

96   Returning the excess enamel to the jar

97   An even glassy surface

edges and back are cleaned carefully with emery and metal polish. When cleaning the edges great care must be taken to rub away from the enamel surface in case the actual enamel edge is chipped (101). The pendant is completed (102) by giving the back a coat of metal lacquer and the addition of a thong or chain.

100   The second firing ▶

98   Drawing with oil

99   Removing the excess powder

101 Cleaning the edges with emery

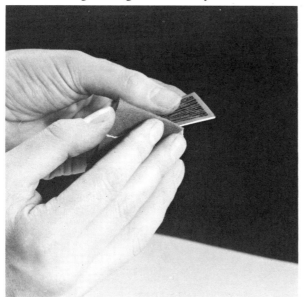

102 The finished pendant

103 This bracelet in red and black enamel is linked with black leather thonging. The black decoration was produced by spattering oil on to the red enamel surface after the first firing and then dusting with black enamel powder before refiring

104 A pendant in tan and black enamels with an adjustable slide

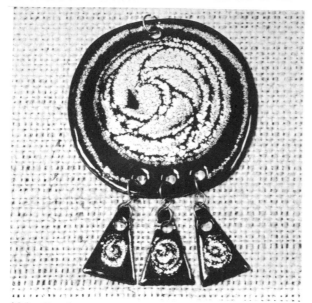

106 Pendants made by children using a sgraffito technique. The second dusting covers the whole piece and a match stick or similar instrument is used to scratch through the powder and expose the first colour

105 Pendant made by a student in black and white enamels

107 Two pendants and a brooch made by students. The brooch is nickel silver with an orange enamelled copper disc attached

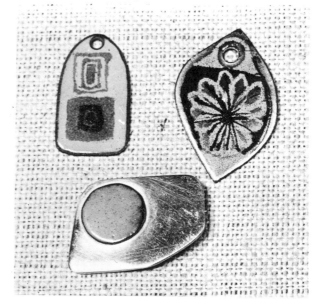

Overleaf

108 Ornaments from S.E. New Guinea, Papua
Left upper Breast ornament of boars tusks bound with barkcloth and twine
Left lower Breast ornament made from a piece of tortoiseshell mounted on a disk of other shell. (Used as currency throughout Melanesia)
Right Charm consisting of a six-lobed piece of wood edged with ground boar's tusks and ornamented with red seeds stuck into gum

109 A necklace and bracelet of bamboo with a necklace of coffee beans and a bracelet of melon seeds

Section 6

Other materials

History again supplies us with a number of other traditional materials which can be used to create fresh and interesting pieces of jewelry.

The following suggestions and illustrations show but a few of the many interesting materials that can be used and the benefit to the student of the search for other unusual materials is inestimable.

The illustrations in figures 108, 115, and 118 show necklaces made by the natives of New Guinea, Papua, Fiji and the Gilbert Islands and the use of this type of natural material is exactly the thing that can be encouraged in the younger age groups to give a basis for future jewelry making.

Seeds

Most children have at some time or other made bracelets or necklaces by threading seeds from a melon and this experience can be taken further by searching for and using other decorative seeds.

A few pennies spent in a shop dealing with poultry food will reveal a marvellous selection of decorative beans and seeds that simply ask to be strung as necklaces.

It is of course possible to dye the beans or seeds with some simple dyestuffs but the vast variety of subtle natural colouring makes this a needless and usually profitless occupation.

Many native trees and plants will provide an extremely interesting source of supply and figure 110 shows among other things a necklace made from beech mast while the dark seeds of lupins and many other garden plants could be used.

The varieties of seeds used by the children who produced the necklaces and bracelets shown in the colour plate will give an idea of the variety of materials of this type that are easily available and will perhaps encourage experiment in this field.

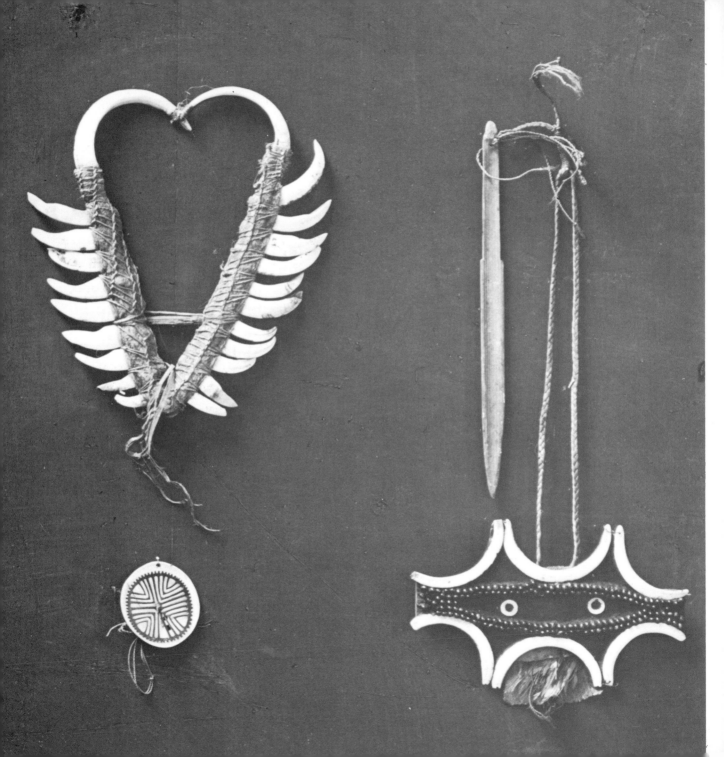

Wood

Though not used in jewelry as widely as one would imagine, wood provides us with a great variety of colour and possibilities for its use.

Exotic hard woods such as ebony, rosewood and walnut are the obvious choice as they are not only beautiful but can be worked almost like metal and cut into sheets and carved without splitting or chipping. Woods of this nature have to be treated almost like sculpture and figure 111 shows a sculpted pendant made from yew.

More basically, however, it is possible to make use of such things as bamboo canes and simple twigs from native trees to produce such things as necklaces and bracelets. Wooden beads can be whittled quite easily from suitable twigs using an ordinary penknife. Beads produced in this way are easily threaded by using a darning needle to push the soft core out of the twig bead and then passing the thread through the resulting hole.

If any difficulty is found, a red-hot wire held in a pair of pliers will solve the problem. Figure 112 shows a string of beads made in this way from elm twigs and also shows the beads in the process of construction. Obviously, the colour of the bark is an important consideration when choosing twigs.

A bamboo cane was simply cut into sections of suitable length and threaded on leather thong to produce the necklace in figure 109. The bracelet in the same illustration was made from pieces cut from a larger section of bamboo and both necklace and bracelet were scorched with the bunsen flame before the thong was added to give a more subtle colour to the finished articles.

◀110 Collection of necklaces made from a variety of materials by students and children

111 A carved pendant in yew wood with an inlay of putty

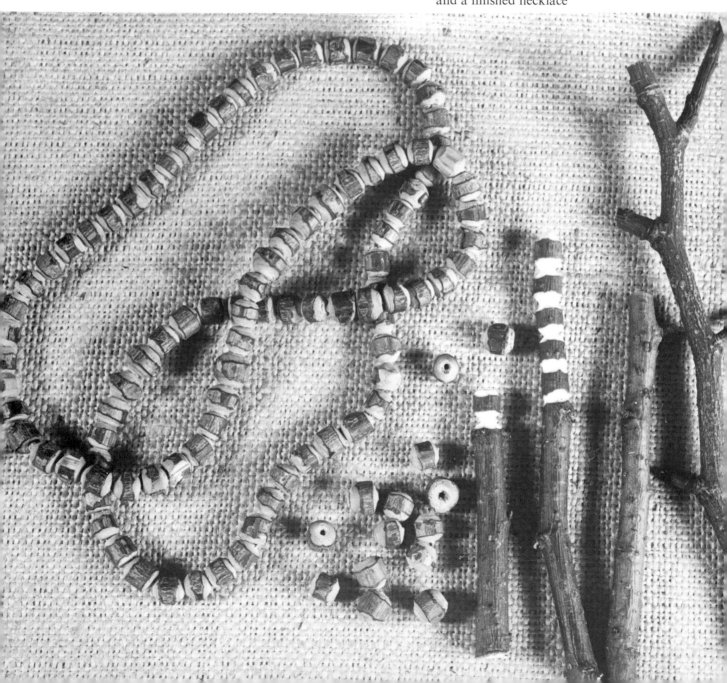

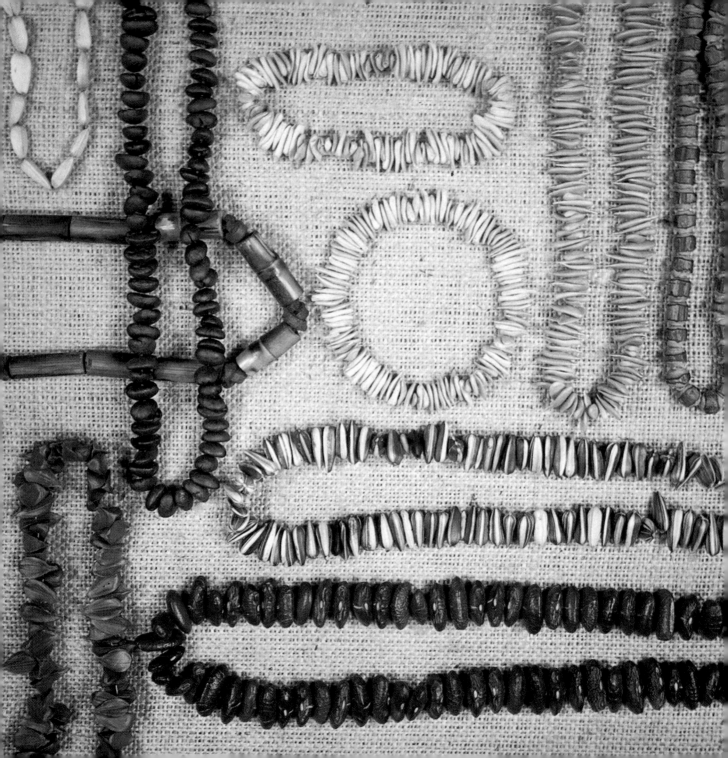

Ivory

Ivory can be used in much the same way as wood but is much stronger and more durable. Good sources for ivory, which is otherwise rather difficult to procure, are old billiard balls and piano keys and these can often be found in junk shops or sale rooms.

The ivory pendant in figure 113 is merely a slice sawn from a small elephant tusk and depends on the basic shape and the pattern of the core for its decorative qualities.

Ivory can be sawn, filed or drilled and polished with emery quite easily and figure 114 shows a number of pieces being prepared for assembly with silver wire to act as links and as binding for the leather thong.

◀ Necklaces and bracelets made from twigs, beans, bamboo, sunflower seeds, melon seeds and beech mast

113　An ivory pendant cut from a small elephant tusk and hung from a black leather thong with silver wire binding

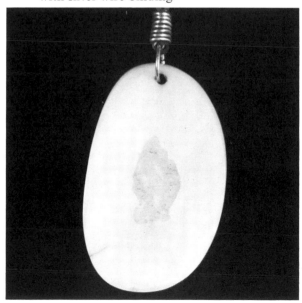

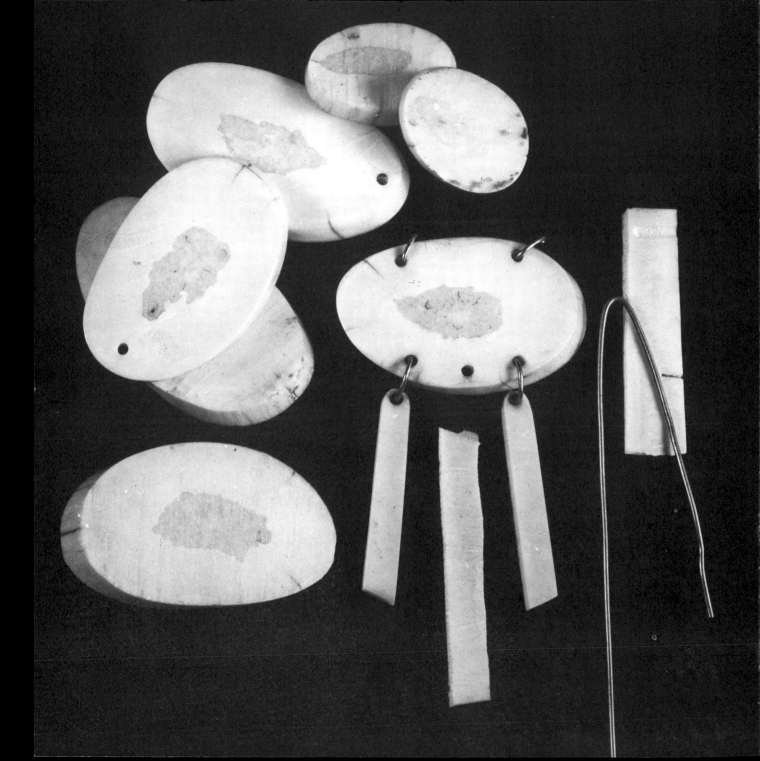

Bone

Primitive man's use of animal and bird bones to produce all kinds of jewelry can be used to illustrate the type of work that can easily be produced from suitable pieces of bone which are either procured from a butcher or found in a more natural state on the hillside or the beach. Many pieces found already bleached by the sun and wind are extremely decorative and will only require slight modifications to make them into interesting articles of jewelry.

Beads can be cut easily from hollow bird bones and the necklace in figure 116 was made from chicken bones cut into lengths with a hacksaw. Figure 117 shows bones being cut into beads in imitation of the examples found at Skara Brae, shown in figures 1 and 3 and the teeth in figure 116 could also be used in much the same way as the boar's tusks in figure 2.

114 Slices of ivory with silver wire and a pendant with ivory drops in process of construction

115 Reddened teeth of the sperm whale suspended from a plaited cord of pandanus leaves. These teeth are used as ceremonial offerings and sometimes as currency. Fiji Islands

116 Bird bones, animal teeth, cowrie shells and a necklace made from chicken bones cut into sections with a hacksaw and varnished

117 Bone beads being produced by cutting sec-tions with a hacksaw ▶

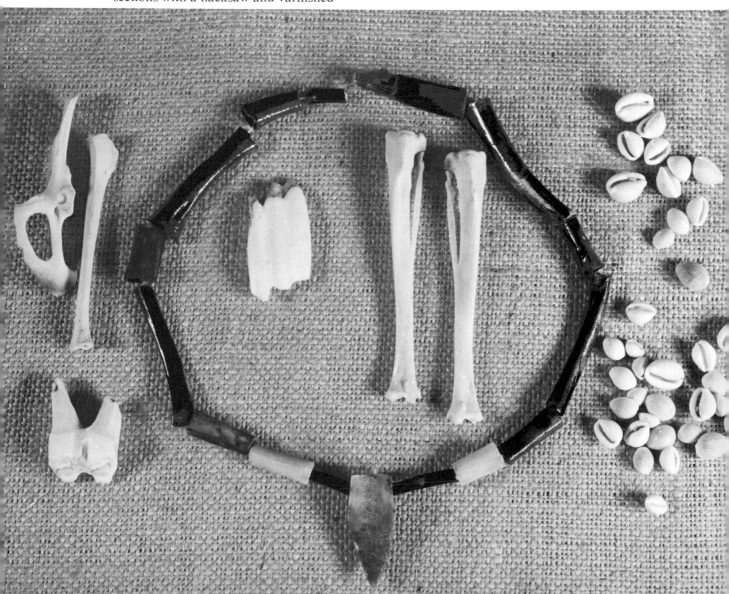

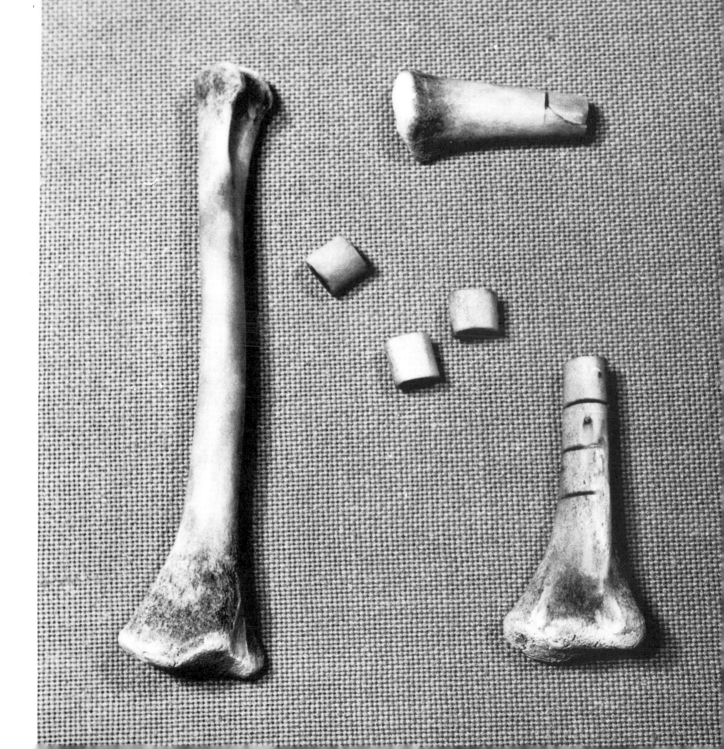

Shells

Shells are among the most attractive of natural 'found objects' and for thousands of years man has used them as decoration and even at times given them a value as money.

It is possible to find many usable shells on most beaches and these can be converted to jewelry by merely stringing them as necklaces. The cowrie shells in figure 116 could be used in this way quite easily by carefully drilling holes through the shells and passing strong twine or nylon thread through them.

The substance known as 'mother of pearl' found inside the shells of oysters and mussels can be cut and sawn with care and the possibilities for its use are vast. The necklace in figure 118 consists of carved pieces of this substance attached to a plaited thong.

◀ 118 Necklace; disks of pearl shell with serrated edges tied to a plaited sinnet cord. Gilbert Islands

Stones

The use of precious stones is beyond the scope of this book and stones are mentioned only because it is possible to collect a great variety of suitable specimens from the beach or river bank.

The sources of sea and river are mentioned because stones found there are liable to be already formed into pebbles that will only need a little more polishing to turn them into extremely attractive objects.

Figure 119 shows a dish of 'tumbled' pebbles. Tumbling is a means of polishing stones where they are placed in a container with water and caraborundum grit and revolved, thus imitating the action of the river grinding the pebbles, until they are smooth. It is possible to construct a fairly simple 'tumbler' and perhaps the geology department of a local museum would provide information on this subject.

More simply it is possible to polish a suitable stone with wet and dry emery paper gradually using a finer and finer grade of paper. This is a long and laborious process but can give remarkably good results.

Stones can be drilled using a hand drill but the two stones in figure 119 had the metal rings attached in a more simple fashion.

The stone was first set in the vice and then a sharp hacksaw was used to cut a groove across the top of it. Into this groove was placed the metal ring and fixed there by using Araldite (epoxy) adhesive. When this sets it is barely visible and the ring is held permanently in position. The addition of a thong or chain allows the stone to be used as a pendant or perhaps a matched pair could be used as earrings.

119 Tumbled pebbles—serpentine, agates and quartz. The pebble on the thong and the one beside it have had silver rings inserted

Jewelry techniques

Simple Jewelry
R. W. Stevens, Studio Vista, London 1966, and Watson-Guptill Publications, New York

Jewelry Making for the Amateur
Klara Lewes, B. T. Batsford, London 1965, and Reinhold, New York

The Technique of Enamelling
Geoffrey Clarke, Francis and Ida Feher, B. T. Batsford, London 1967, and Watson-Guptill Publications, New York

The Design and Creation of Jewelry
Robert von Neuman, Pitman and Son, London 1962

Enamelling
Lewis F. Day, B. T. Batsford 1907 (out of print)

Practical Enamelling and Jewelry Work
Brian Newble, Studio Vista, London

Jewlry and Sculpture through Unit Construction
Patricia Meyerowitz, Studio Vista, London

How to Make Modern Jewelry
Charles J. Martin and Victor D'Amico, The Museum of Modern Art

Jewelry Making
D. Kenneth Winebrenner, International Textbook Company, Pennsylvania

Jewelry and Enamelling
Greta Pack, D. Van Nostrand Company, New York, N.Y.

Handwrought Jewelry
Lois E. Franke, McKnight and McKnight Publishing Company, Bloomington, Illinois

Enamelling on Copper
Thomas C. Thompson Company, Highland Park, Illinois

Enamelling
Kenneth F. Bates, The World Publishing Company, Cleveland and New York

The Art of Enameling or Enameling can be Fun
Mizi Otten and Kathe Berl, New York

Introducing Enamelling
Valerie Conway, B. T. Batsford, London, Watson-Guptill, New York

Design and form

Teaching Design and Form
Gunner Sneum, B. T. Batsford, London 1965

Basic Design: The Dynamics of Visual Form
Maurice de Sausmarez, Studio Vista, London

The Nature of Design
David Pye, Studio Vista, London

You are an Artist
Fred Gettings, Paul Hamlyn, London

How to Design Monograms and Symbols
Curtiss Sprague, Brigman Publishers Inc, Pelham, N.Y.

Suppliers in Great Britain

Copper

J. & A. Dunn Ltd,
Blair Street,
Edinburgh

H. W. Landon & Brothers,
9–12 Bartholomew Row,
Birmingham 5

London Metal Warehouses Ltd,
15 Edgware Road,
London W.2

J. Smith & Sons (Clerkenwell),
50 St Johns Square,
London E.C.1

Henry Righton & Co. Ltd,
70 Pentonville Road,
London N.1

H. Rollet & Co. Ltd,
6 Chesham Place,
London S.W.1

+ Local electrical and plumbing suppliers

Jewelry Tools

Charles Cooper Ltd,
92–93 Hatton Garden,
London E.C.1

E. Gray & Son Ltd,
12–16 Clerkenwell Road,
London E.C.1

Herring Morgan & Southon Ltd,
9 Berwick Street,
London W.1
(also supply jewelry findings)

George Panton & Sons,
Buchanan Street,
Glasgow

Precious Metals

Johnson Matthey & Co. Ltd,
78 Hatton Garden,
London E.C.1
also Victoria Street, Birmingham

Enamelling requisites

Fred Aldous Ltd,
37 Lever Street,
Manchester M60 IUX

Art and Crafts Unlimited,
49 Shelton Street,
London W.C.2

Enamelaire Ltd,
61B High Street,
Watford, Herts

W. J. Hutton,
285 Icknield Street,
Hockley,
Birmingham

Schauer Enamels, Thomson and Joseph Ltd,
46 Watling Street,
Radlet, Hertfordshire

Bernard W. E. Webber Ltd,
Webcot Works,
Alfred Street,
Finton, Stoke on Trent

Suppliers in the U.S.A.

Gold, silver, copper, tools, findings, enamels
Allcraft,
22 West 48th Street,
New York,
N.Y. 10036

Anchor Tool & Supply Company Inc,
12 John Street,
New York,
N.Y. 10038

Copper, findings
American Handicraft Company Inc,
20 West 14th Street,
New York,
N.Y.

Findings
Krieger & Dranoff,
44 West 47th Street,
New York,
N.Y. 10036

Silver
Hagstoz & Son,
709 Sansom Street,
Philadelphia, Pennsylvania

Enamels, enamelling supplies
Thomas C. Thompson Company,
Highland Park,
Illinois

Stones
Nathan Gem & Pearl Company Inc,
18 East 48th Street,
New York,
N.Y. 10017

International Gem,
15 Maiden Lane,
New York,
N.Y. 10038

Stones and rough material
A & S Gem and Mineral Co,
611 Broadway,
New York,
N.Y.

The numerals in *italic* refer to illustrations